First World War
and Army of Occupation
War Diary
France, Belgium and Germany

4 CAVALRY DIVISION
Divisional Troops
16 Brigade Royal Horse Artillery
1 January 1917 - 24 February 1918

WO95/1158/2

The Naval & Military Press Ltd
www.nmarchive.com
Published in association with The National Archives

Published by

The Naval & Military Press Ltd

Unit 10 Ridgewood Industrial Park,

Uckfield, East Sussex,

TN22 5QE England

Tel: +44 (0) 1825 749494

www.naval-military-press.com

www.nmarchive.com

This diary has been reprinted in facsimile from the original. Any imperfections are inevitably reproduced and the quality may fall short of modern type and cartographic standards.

© **Crown Copyright**
Images reproduced by permission of The National Archives, London, England, 2015.

Contents

Document type	Place/Title	Date From	Date To
Heading	WO95/1158/2		
Heading	1917 4th Cavalry Division 16th Brigade R.H.A. & 1917 Jan-1918 Feb From Indian Cav Div As 1 Bde RHA Box 1170 To 4 Army Troops 1158		
Heading	War Diary of Headquarters, 1st Indian R. H. A. Brigade. From 1st January 1917 To 31st January 1917		
War Diary	St Valery	01/01/1917	19/03/1917
War Diary	Buigny St McLoux Canaples	20/03/1917	20/03/1917
War Diary	Albert	21/03/1917	21/03/1917
War Diary	Ervillers	28/03/1917	31/03/1917
Heading	Headquarters, 16th R. H. A. Brigade. From 1st to 30th April 1917.		
Miscellaneous	Issued to Section		
War Diary	Ervillers	01/04/1917	01/05/1917
War Diary	Le Transloy	10/05/1917	10/05/1917
War Diary	Moislains	12/05/1917	12/05/1917
War Diary	Boucly	13/05/1917	13/05/1917
War Diary	Caulincourt	14/05/1917	23/05/1917
War Diary	Roisel	23/05/1917	24/05/1917
War Diary	Hervilly	25/05/1917	10/07/1917
War Diary	Athies	11/07/1917	11/07/1917
War Diary	Villers-Carbonnel	13/07/1917	30/11/1917
War Diary	Villers Foucon	01/12/1917	02/12/1917
War Diary	Athies	07/12/1917	07/12/1917
War Diary	Jaencourt	09/12/1917	30/12/1917
War Diary	Athies	01/01/1918	31/01/1918
War Diary	Somme and France	01/02/1918	24/02/1918

WO 95/11581/2

1917
4TH CAVALRY DIVISION

16TH BRIGADE R.H.A.
&
~~DIVL AMMUNITION COLUMN~~
~~JAN - DEC 1917~~

1917. JAN — 1918. FEB

FROM INDIAN CAV DIV
As 1 BDE RHA   Box 1170

TO 4 ARMY TROOPS

1158

SERIAL NO. 49.

Confidential

War Diary

of

HEADQUARTERS, 1st INDIAN R.H.A. BRIGADE.

FROM 1st JANUARY 1917 TO 31st JANUARY 1917

Army Form C. 2118.

1st Indian R.H. A. Bde — Confidential

WAR DIARY or Intelligence Summary
Head Quarters 4th Cavalry Division
INTELLIGENCE SUMMARY.
(Erase heading not required.)

No. 61

Place	Date	Hour	Summary of Events and Information	Remarks and references to Appendices
JANUARY 1917 ST VALERY	1st		Major W. P. PAYNTER R.H.A. O.B. RHA awarded D.S.O. London Gazette dated 1 Jany 1917 (W)	
	2nd		Section of D.A.C. left FRESSENNEVILLE to join up with U Bty R.H.A. (W)	
	3rd		"A" Bty R.H.A. billet at LONGPRÉ en route to SALLENELLE to rejoin Division (W)	
	4th		A Bty billet at TOEUFLES (W)	
	5th		A Bty march to SALLENELLE (W)	
	5th		Q Bty to AIRAINES en route to 1st Army Arty School, taking les of D.A.C. (W)	
	6th		U Bty left AMIENOIS to join XIV Corps (W)	
	8th		A Bty R.H.A. re armed with 13 pdr Egyptian. 18 pdrs returned same day (W)	
	14th		13 pdr Ammn drawn to complete A Bty. D.A.C. & R.O.A. Park (W)	
	26th		B. CLARKE. WILLIAMS attached U Bty admitted Hôspl (wounded by (W) Native Arty Fire)	

31 January 1917

F Westropp Lieut RHA
ADJUTANT,
1st INDIAN R.H.A. BRIGADE.

Army Form C. 2118.

1ST INDIAN R.H.A. BRIGADE H.Q. 4th Cavalry Division

WAR DIARY
INTELLIGENCE SUMMARY.
(Erase heading not required.)

No 62

Place	Date	Hour	Summary of Events and Information	Remarks and references to Appendices
FEBY	1917 4th/12 6/12		Lt C. WEST. R.H.A joined and posted to 'A' By R.H.A.	
	"		Lt R.R. HOARE R.H.A. joined and posted to 'U' By R.H.A	
X	2nd		2/Lt S.W. LEWIS R.F.A. Div¹ Amm¹ Col⁰ evacuated to England sick and struck off strength	
R	7		Lt J.C. ELLIS, R.F.A. attached A By having been returned to England is struck off strength	
	7		2/Lt St J.G. KEMM appointed to R.H.A.	
E	11		Lt C.N.G. TURNER R.H.A joined and posted to 'Q' By R.H.A	
	23		Sgt KILLEEN Div¹ Amm¹ⁿ Col⁰ⁿ Commissioned & posted to 62ⁿᵈ Bde Div¹ Arty (left on 23ʳᵈ)	
L	24		Title of R.H.A Brigade changed to 16ᵗʰ Brigade R.H.A.	
A	25ᵗʰ		Lt WEST. Lt HOARE and Lt TURNER attended 4ᵗʰ Course at Cavalry School R.H.A School	
	25ᵗʰ	11.45 pm	Orders received that 'A' By and Section (Guns & S.A.A.) of 'D' By to be held in readiness to accompany LUCKNOW Brigade into the Line	
V	26ᵗʰ	3.00 am	Orders that 'A' By 1 Section of D.A Col⁰ⁿ to be at MOYENNEVILLE at 10.30 a.m.	
			Battery moved, picking up the 4 guns which were at 48ᵗʰ Mobile Workshops at BEAUCHAMPS being overhauled	
S	27ᵗʰ		Sgt FORD 'A' By R.H.A Commissioned and posted to 16ᵗʰ Bde Arty	
	27ᵗʰ		1 Gun Section of D.A. Park moved to I ANZAC Corps Ammn Park	

FIELD 28/2/1917

J.F.Wcott Lieut R.H.A.
Adj¹ 16ᵗʰ Brigade R.H.A.

R.H.A. BRIGADE

16th Brigade R.H.A. Hear Qtrs

WAR DIARY
INTELLIGENCE SUMMARY.
(Erase heading not required.)

Army Form C. 2118.
63

MARCH 1917

Place	Date	Hour	Summary of Events and Information	Remarks and references to Appendices
ST VALLERY	19th		Division left St Vallery billeting area for 5th Army Area.	
BUIGNY ST MCLOUX CANAPLES	20R 21st		Billeted night of 19/20 at Buigny St Meloux Billeted night of 20/21 at Canaples	
ALBERT	26.12		Division moved to Camp 1500x N.E. of Albert R.H.A Bde H. Q. with Q and U Batteries moved to ERVILLERS to join 7th Division at forkl	
ERVILLERS			R.H.A Column moved to ACHIET Le GRAND Q + U Batteries moved into action just E. of ERVILLERS close to (67) A Bty 18Ld Major Emeo put I/c of ERVILLERS with R.H.A. Bde Hd Qrs. Lt Col ROCHFORT BOYD D.S.O. R.H.A. took over command of A.Q - U Batteries as "C" Group of Y/10 Division - these Batteries previously have attacked to 91st? Bde R.H.A	
	30R		U Battery moved position 500x east Q and A Batteries moved forward about 1 mile (?)	
	31			

FW Coote Lt R.H.A
Adjt. @ 16th Bde R.H.A
1st Cavalry Division

1/4/17

Serial No: **49**

Headquarters, 16th R.H.A. Brigade.

From 1st to 30th April 1917.

Daily list of

in Adjutan

Issued to Section

From whom.	No. and date of letter received.

Army Form C. 2118.

WAR DIARY

H.Q. Qr, 16th Brigade, R.H.A. No. 104
INTELLIGENCE SUMMARY.

(Erase heading not required.)

Place	Date	Hour	Summary of Events and Information	Remarks and references to Appendices
ERILLERS	1917 8th		Batteries still in action under 7th Division. /JEW	
	9th		Brigade came under orders of 62nd Division /JEW 4th Cavalry Division to be prepared to move at any time after 4 hrs	
	10th		Division to be in position of readiness at 4.30 am — Report evolve L'HOMME MORT /JEW 8pm Batteries were returning to bivouacs — Attack having been postponed. 7 am Division returned to bivouacs — Batteries recalled to their wagon lines. Division was under 1 hour notice. Orders received that Division would be in position of readiness as yesterday at 8 am /JEW	
	11th		About 7 am SIALKOT Bde with Q Battery moved up behind ECOUST, and shortly came under 4.2 How and 77mm fire — Lt THORNHILL Sgt HEATH and Dr GREVES being wounded.	
		4pm	Division returned to bivouacs about 4.30pm Information that R.H.A. Bde were directly under V Corps & that Batteries placed at disposal of 62 Division — Batteries to go into action on 12th /JEW	
	13th		Division returned to BaR area, leaving R.H.A. Bde in the line /JEW	
	16th		"A" Battery R.H.A. went out of action & rejoined the MHOW Bde. /JEW	
	24th		100 Remounts arrived at Fosseux for R.H.A. Bde. 50 sent to A Battery R.H.A and the	

Army Form C. 2118.

WAR DIARY
or
INTELLIGENCE SUMMARY. N° 64
(Erase heading not required.)

Instructions regarding War Diaries and Intelligence
Summaries are contained in F. S. Regs., Part II
and the Staff Manual respectively. Title pages
will be prepared in manuscript.

Place	Date	Hour	Summary of Events and Information	Remarks and references to Appendices
ERVILLERS	26th		Remainder sent to the Baths temporarily - pending instruction by CC Cavalry /EW Remounts sent to Q the Batteries and D.a.c. Echelon /EW During the month the Brigade availed in several attacks on HINDENBURG line. Night firing taking place every night - Bivouacs changed continually - The Chestnut Troop took a large number of horses owing to the very hard cold weather, since they had been in the line. /EW Brigade - (less 'A' Battery) still in the line under 62 Division /EW	
	30th		Field 30/4/17	

Yeatstone Lt R.H.A
Adjutant Brigade
16

2353 Wt W2544/1454 700,000 5/15 D. D. & L. A.D.S.S./Forms/C. 2118.

4 Cav. Army Form C. 2118.

WAR DIARY

Head Quarters or, 16 Brigade RHA
INTELLIGENCE SUMMARY No 65

(Erase heading not required.)

Place	Date	Hour	Summary of Events and Information	Remarks and references to Appendices
May 1917				
ERVILLERS	1st		RHA Brigade (less 'A' Battery) still in action /JES	
LE TRANSLOY	10th		Brigade (less 'A' Bty) marched to near SUCRERIE (N.W. of LE TRANSLOY) Units marched independently.	
	11th		Divisional Ammunition Column completed to establishment of Ammunition from Cavalry Corps Dump, the balance of the Dump, together with all ammunition from Divisional Ammunition Park being returned to Ammunition Railheads or Dumps /JES	
MOISLAINS	12th		Brigade marched to MOISLAINS /JES	
BOUCLY	13th		Brigade marched to BOUCLY /JES	
CAULINCOURT	14th		Batteries marched to CAULINCOURT Div: Ammn: Colm to CAVIGNY FARM (near CAULINCOURT) /JES	
	15th		Brigade detached. One marched to SMALL FOOT FARM (yds SE of VENDELLES) 'D' and 'U' Batteries put one Section each into the Line, in relief of B/159 and C/159 respectively /JES	
	16th		'D' and 'U' Batteries put. remaining sections into the Line and came under the orders of Lt Col DAWSON R.F.A. Lieut BURNINGHAM joined Hd Qrs from Div Ammte Colmn, in relief of Capt	

D. D. & L.

Army Form C. 2118.

WAR DIARY
or
INTELLIGENCE SUMMARY.   No 6 5/A
(Erase heading not required.)

Place	Date	Hour	Summary of Events and Information	Remarks and references to Appendices
May 1917 Continued	10th		Bawkins to "Q" Bty RHA /FW	
	19th		Col Rochfort-Boyd D.S.O. RHA took over command of RIGHT GROUP, 5th Cavalry Divisional Artillery (consisting of "Q" and "U" Batteries RHA, N and X Batteries and H and B Batteries Royal Canadian Horse Arty) /FW	
	21st		Divl Ammn Colm attached 2 J.S Dragoons to Q and U Batteries to replace those of A & J Company recalled /FW	
	22nd		"U" Battery brought one Section out of action to wagon lines, being relieved by A/295. Relief completed 23rd /FW	
			"A" Battery reld 3 guns into action in relief of A/295 /FW	
ROISEL	23rd		Col Rochfort Boyd handed over Command of RIGHT GROUP to Lt Col Stirling/RHA "A" Bty remaining 3 guns in action (by one Bde ??) Head Qrs moved to ROISEL (Head Qrs of 295 Brigade R.F.A.) /FW	
	24th	9 am	Col Rochfort Boyd took over command of 4th Cavalry Divisional Arty consisting of HQ Batteries RHA, B/295 C/295 and D/295	
HERVILLY	25th		Those Head Qrs moved to HERVILLY /FW	

FIELD
31–5–1917

FW Scotrope Lt Col
Captain 16th Bde RHA
Acting 16th Bde RHA

Army Form C. 2118.

HEAD QUARTERS, 16th BRIGADE, R.H.A.

WAR DIARY
INTELLIGENCE SUMMARY.
(Erase heading not required.)

No. 66

Instructions regarding War Diaries and Intelligence Summaries are contained in F. S. Regs., Part II, and the Staff Manual respectively. Title pages will be prepared in manuscript.

Place	Date 1917	Hour	Summary of Events and Information	Remarks and references to Appendices
	June 1st		Corpl. H.W. HUGGINS, D.S.O. M.C. "U" Battery RHA left for B/175 RFA /EES	
	12th		H.A. Col. moved from DOUCY to just South of HANCOURT /EES	
	15th		1 Gun "U" Battery RHA went into the line attached to 5th Cavalry Division /EES	
	16th		" " " " " " " "	
	17th		1 Gun of C/295 (attached) sent to Brae /EES	
	19th		"U" Battery RHA came out of action /EES	
	20th		2/Lt. TRIPP posted to 1st Division Arty on Commission /EES	
	25th		Lt. MAUDE admitted Hospital - injured Collar bone - done on duty /EES	
	26th		Lt. J. F. FLEMMING joined "U" Bty. from R.M.A. /EES	
	28th		Lt. L.P. HUGGINS RFA (T) joined "A" Bty on posting from 2nd Army Ht. Arti. Bde /EES	
	26th		2/Lt. H.W. HAYLEY R.F.A. left Cheshire troop for 30th Division /EES	
	29th		C/295 RFA attached from 3rd Cavy Division /EES	
	-		2 Heavy Trench Mortars attached from Ht. Army Schools /EES	
	30th		2 Medium Trench Batteries attached from 59 Division /EES	
	30th		"U" Bty RHA into action just east of TEMPLEUX /EES	

30/6/17

J. Soothey [?] Lt Col RHA
Cmdg 16th RHA Bde
Oct. 16th RHA Bde

16th Bde R H A

WAR DIARY or **INTELLIGENCE SUMMARY**
Army Form C. 2118.

(Erase heading not required.)

Instructions regarding War Diaries and Intelligence Summaries are contained in F. S. Regs., Part II and the Staff Manual respectively. Title pages will be prepared in manuscript.

Place	Date	Hour	Summary of Events and Information	Remarks and references to Appendices
HERMIES	2-7-17		Early this morning hostile exploded mine on Railway down with satisfying results	
	6-7-17		Sgt Rotherham "A" Bty Commissioned Forces B" Division	
	8"		Canadian Cavalry Brigade raided Aeroplane Trench "A" "Q" & "U" Btys Assisted	
	9"		Corporal Adam's "U" Bty Commissioned	
	10"		7th Cavalry Division relieved by 34th Division	
ATHIES	11"		Bde H.Q moved to ATHIES. "Q" Bty marched to Wagon Lies at Hamencourt	
			"A" & "U" in action under 34th Division	
VILLERS- CARBONNEL	13"		Bde Head Quarters moved to VILLERS-CARBONNEL	
	16"		Sgt Sinnett Q Bty R.H.A Commissioned Posted 154th Division	
	23"		"Q" Battery went into action under 34th Divisional Artillery	
	24"		Wagon Lines moved to BOUGLY	
	25"		Lieut T. Sheridan of the United States Medical Corps joined for duty as M.O.	
	26		Divisional Horse Show	
			Lieut G. Sandeman reported from 20th Division Posted to "U" Bty	

31-7-17

E J Hutchins Lt Col
a/Adjt 16 HRA RHA

WAR DIARY
Head Quarters 16th Bryade RHA
INTELLIGENCE SUMMARY.

No 6 8

Army Form C. 2118.

Place	Date	Hour	Summary of Events and Information	Remarks and references to Appendices
VILLERS CARBONNEL	August 1917			
	22nd		2/Lt S.H. JACKSON R.F.A. (S.R.) joins from Base posted to 'A' Battery R.H.A. JEW	
	22nd		No 253 A.O.C./Arm Sjt Maj WILLIAMS G., 87760 Sjt BURROWS G., 77296 Sjt PHILLIMORE P., all of 'Q' Bty wounded in action by Arty fire JEW	
	26th		Lieut Bt/J. G. KEMM. R.H.A., 77538 Sjt WATERTON S., 52841 Sjt VENABLES A. 69641 Sjt TURNER R.H., all of 'U' Baty R.H.A wounded in action by Arty fire JEW	
	27th		2/Lt JACKSON R.F.A. Greene JEW	
	27th		Lieut C.R. JOHNSTON, R.F.A joins from Base posted to 'A' Bty R.H.A. JEW	
	30th		Lt JACKSON joins 'U' Bty on posting from 'A' Bty R.H.A JEW	
	31st		Batteries still in the line under 3rd Divisional Arty. JEW	

Tries 1/9/1917

J E Westropp Lt RHA
Adjutant 16th Bde RHA

Army Form C. 2118.

Serial No. 49

WAR DIARY
16th Brigade or R.H.A. Head Quarters
INTELLIGENCE SUMMARY.
No 69

Place	Date	Hour	Summary of Events and Information	Remarks and references to Appendices
VILLERS CARBONNEL	September 1917 3rd 5th		Lt S. H. JACKSON RFA left "U" Bty for 18th Divisional Arty HQrs 2 Lt G D CASTELLI R.H.A. and 2 Lt J BOSTOCK R.H.A. reported 16 R.H.A. Bde and posted	
		8th 9th	to "A" and "U" Battery respectively HQrs Establishment of rifles increased from 36 to 94 per Battery HQrs 2 Lt J. G. KEMM R.H.A. "U" Bty R.H.A. awarded Military Cross - Authy IInd Army No	
		10th 12th 21st 24th 26th	HR 716 dt. 9.9.17 / HQrs Lt J. G. KEMM invalided to England "wounded" HQrs Lt ALMACK R.H.A. awarded Military Cross HQrs Ammunition – Establishment amended to 50% HE and 50% Shrapnel HQrs "Q" Battery R.H.A. out of line – remains with Wagon Lines at BOUVY HQrs Horse Weekly – Establishment reduced from 70 to 40 per Battery HQrs	
	30.9.1917.			

J. Eustropoulevil R.H.A.
Adjutant 16 Bde R.H.A.

Army Form C. 2118.

44.

WAR DIARY
INTELLIGENCE SUMMARY.

16th Brigade R.F.A. Hqrs Quarters No 40

(Erase heading not required.)

Place	Date	Hour	Summary of Events and Information	Remarks and references to Appendices
October 1917	1st	—	Capt. G.P. Simpson, M.C. 'Q' Bty. RHA left for 1st Division	
VILLERS CARBONNEL	2nd	—	Lt. T.G.P. Winmill joined from 78th Army Bde R.F.A. and Posted as Orderly Officer. Appts to Rita from date of joining. Authy H.Q. 51st D/1190/101 dated 27/9/17	Yes
	3rd	—	Lt. Lenanton Q. Bty apptd a/Captain — vice Simpson. Authy Bewdey Corps No AMS/321/141 dated 24/10/17	Yes
	4th		2.L. F.M.A. Wood R.F.A. B'Ta Col posted to 29th Div. Arty as recorded in Command of 'a' Bty R.F.A.	Yes
	14th		'Q' Bty moved to St. Christ.	Yes
	15th		'U' Bty rejoins from 2nd Division + relieved at Le Mesnil.	Yes
	19th		B.S.M. Hodges 'A' Bty Commissions. Posted to 5B-20 Div Arty	Yes
	20th		'A' Bty to Athies	Yes
	21st		All Guns in Brigade inspected by I.O.O.	Yes
	24th		" " B/a Col Batteries inspected by I.O.O.	Yes
			Lt. C.S.N. Turner Rita posted to 41 Div Arty as record in Command of Battery R.F.A.	Yes

11/11/1917

J.E. Soothropp ?? R.F.A.
A/ D.?. R.H.A. Bde

Army Form C. 2118.

WAR DIARY
16th Brigade R.H.A. H.Q. &c
INTELLIGENCE SUMMARY.
(Erase heading not required.)

November 1917

Place	Date	Hour	Summary of Events and Information	Remarks and references to Appendices
Villers Carbonnel	3rd		Orders for Major W.P. Paynter DSO RHA to assume Command of 16th Army Bde RHA. /EW	
	10th		Brigade HQ moved to ATHIES. /EW	
	11th		Orders received that Brigade would move to ALLAINES area on night of 14/15 and to come under Orders of III Corps /EW	
	14th		RHA Bde (less 'U' Bty RHA) moved to VAUX WOOD	
	16th		A+Q Battery fire put into position /EW	
	19th		Bde left VAUX WOOD for E34.d (57c) /EW	
	20th		Bde attached to 6th Division for attack on CAMBRAI. Bombardment opened at 6.20 a.m. About 10.15 a.m the Brigade with 111th Bty RFA attached came under orders of 29th Division Arty and ordered to advance by Brigades tracks to L32.a. Arrived at once to L33.a where they remained for 2 days then moved to L27 Central — Hd Qrs d MARCOING /EW	
	23rd		Hd Qrs moved to L26.d.9.5 (57c) /EW	
	28th		Came out of action and Bde moved to Q13.c /EW	
	29th		Bde moved to old Bivouac in ATHIES area /EW	
	30		Division concentrated at P3.d (62c) and moved to E16.c 2.3 Bde Hd Qr with RHQ 4th Bde /EW	

Lewealt[?] Capt RHA
Acg I/c 16th Bde RHA
1/12/1917

Army Form C. 2118.

WAR DIARY
or
INTELLIGENCE SUMMARY.

Hd Qr 16th Bde RHA 4 Cavalry Division
No 4.

Place	Date	Hour	Summary of Events and Information	Remarks and references to Appendices
RECORDS 1914	1/9/14		Bde moves forward to Advance Report Centre with Div Hd Qr Report Centre at E 5. c - Batteries in action at W 30	
VILLERS FAUCON			Col Rochfort Boyd DSO wounded in action - to Hospital Maj E E Rich "U" Bty RHA wounded in action. (died same day). Bde Commanded by Maj Dudley, A Bty RHA from evening of 1st. 2/Lt Forster joins from 5th Division Ammunition Park 1st "U" Bty RHA 2/Lt Anglesea Sandels joins from 126 Bde RFA posted to B Bty RHA	
ATHIES	2nd		Bde rejoins 4 Cavalry Div area. 2/Lt Woodroffe. J.W. joins from "D"Bty" RHA posted to A Bty RHA 2/Lt	
JAENCOURT	9.2		Bde moved under Major Stanley to join 2nd Div Arty Hd Qr Batteries into action at L 32.c (A B H) Scarletts Group (Q B H) Mellors Group (U B H) Stirlings Group	
			Hd Qr in Sunken Road at L 32 a 5. 3 Information received from Base that Col Rochfort Boyd had died from wounds on 4th inst.	

Army Form C. 2118.

WAR DIARY
or
INTELLIGENCE SUMMARY.

No Y/3

(Erase heading not required.)

Place	Date	Hour	Summary of Events and Information	Remarks and references to Appendices
	12		2/L Dunlop. D. joins "V" B/y R.H.A. New.	
	14		Lt Col J.G.B ALLARDYCE joins B/de and assumed Command of R.H.A B/de from 39" Div Arty Hd.Q.	
	17		Maj A.Q. ARCHDALE assumed Command of V. B/y R.H.A New	
	21		Maj Dudley. A B/y R.H.A took over STIRLINGS GROUP New	
	30		Hd. Qr. R.H.A B/de reports Dit/th Op at ATHIES. New Batteries remaining in action on account of snow New	
	31/12/1918		Died	

Everhopp Cap! R.H.A
Ewo R.H.A 16th Bde R.H.A

ADQRS. 16TH BDE R.H.A. 4th CAVALRY DIVISION. Army Form C. 2118.

WAR DIARY
INTELLIGENCE SUMMARY.
(Erase heading not required.)

Instructions regarding War Diaries and Intelligence Summaries are contained in F.S. Regs., Part II. and the Staff Manual respectively. Title pages will be prepared in manuscript.

Place	Date	Hour	Summary of Events and Information	Remarks and references to Appendices
JANUARY 1918.				
ATHIES	1st		"J" and "U" Batteries still in action. "Q" Battery resting in BERNES.	
	12th		Major A.W. Van Straubenzee, D.S.O. R.H.A. joined Bde and assumed command of "J" R.H.A.	
	14th		Major A.N.W. Bradley, R.H.A. proceeded from "A" R.H.A. to assume command of 291st Bde R.F.A.	
	15th		Lt. A.C. Donitor, R.H.A. posted from "J" R.H.A. to 55th Armd. Artillery.	
	16th		Right Half "A" Bty withdrew from line to Wagon lines at HAMELET.	
	17th		Remaining guns of "A" R.H.A. withdrawn to Wagon lines at HAMELET.	
	"		"U" R.H.A. moved out of action and marched to Wagon Lines at BERNES-COULAINCOURT.	
	18th		Lt. T.W. WOODROFFE "A" Bty R.H.A. invalided to England.	
	19th		Capt Thompson "A" R.H.A. Commissions and posted to 36th Armd Arty.	
	21st		Lt. C.W. ALMACK, "Q" R.H.A. awarded Bar to Military Cross (Mily A.M. & Cat. Life Ams 513/103)	
	23rd		Lt. R.A. GRAY, M.C. joined from 28th Army Bde R.F.A. and assumed command of D.A. Column	
	31st		ADQRS. still in ATHIES, "A" Bty in HAMELET, "Q" Bty in BERNES, "U" Bty in CAULAINCOURT, and D.A.Column in DEVISE.	

IN THE FIELD
31-1-1918

J. Gummell. L.R.H.A.
for ADJT.
16th Bde R.H.A.

Army Form C. 2118.

WAR DIARY of 16th Bde R.H.A.
INTELLIGENCE SUMMARY. February 1918

(Erase heading not required.)

Place	Date	Hour	Summary of Events and Information	Remarks and references to Appendices
SOMME area FRANCE	1st–21st		4th CAN DIV AN Bde. During this period the brigade was distributed tactically as follows:— H.Q. Remained at BOUVINCOURT until moved up into	
	21st.		Battle H.Q. of Right Group – stores left at W.L. at BOUVINCOURT.–	
			The Chestnut Troop, in huts and stables at HAMELET, was in readiness to man their anti-tank position in front of HESBECOURT should occasion arise – A good deal of open warfare training was done; and for	
	12th/13th		two nights the guns were in action at VADENCOURT, participating in a raid on the German trenches.–	
			Q. Bty. was in anti-tank reserve at BERNES, and also did a certain amount of open warfare training. The battery took part in the raid on the German trenches, after which the guns were withdrawn to	
	12th/13th		BERNES – U Bty. remained at their W.L. at CAULAINCOURT for the first	
	9th		week, training for open warfare, and was then moved up into action E. of Fir Copse to register for the above-mentioned raid, after which	
	13th		they withdrew to their W.L. for a few days – They then relieved N Bty.	
	19th		in action, S.E. of VENDELLES –	

(continued)

(2 pages)

Army Form C. 2118.

WAR DIARY of 16th Bde R.H.A.

INTELLIGENCE SUMMARY. February 1918 - (continued)

(Erase heading not required.)

Instructions regarding War Diaries and Intelligence Summaries are contained in F. S. Regs., Part II. and the Staff Manual respectively. Title pages will be prepared in manuscript.

Place	Date	Hour	Summary of Events and Information	Remarks and references to Appendices
SOMME area FRANCE	1st – 28th		D.A.C. remained at ATHIES, where driving drill and general training of personnel were carried out. Casualties - Personnel & horses.	
	22nd		2nd Lieut C.A. Holmes joined the Chestnut Troop, and took over the Centre Section vice Lieut. G.R. Johnston, who became adjutant at Bde H.Q.	
	25th		All the Indian drivers of V and Q batteries left the brigade for	
	24th		MARSEILLES base. Killed or wounded — nil.	

(28-2-18)

E.M. MacLeod, R.H.A.
Adjt. 16th Bde R.H.A.

www.ingramcontent.com/pod-product-compliance
Lightning Source LLC
Chambersburg PA
CBHW082359170426
43191CB00048B/2116